MW00949598

# My
# LASER FILE
# Log Book

## Personal Information

Name: _____

Phone: _____

Address: _____

_____

Email: _____

## Book Information

Book Number: _____

Book Start Date: _____

Book End Date: _____

| | FILE/PROJECT NAME | | |
|---|---|---|---|

| | ORDER DATE | | WHERE ORDERED |
|---|---|---|---|

| | FILE COST | | CLIENT |
|---|---|---|---|

| | LASER ACTION | SCORE ☐ | ENGRAVE ☐ | CUT ☐ |
|---|---|---|---|---|

| | RUN TIME | ✔ FINISHED |
|---|---|---|

## SET-UP

| | MACHINE USED |
|---|---|

| | SETTINGS | SPEED | POWER | LPI |
|---|---|---|---|---|

| | NO. OF PASSES |
|---|---|

| | MATERIAL SIZE | ‖‖‖ THICKNESS |
|---|---|---|

## MATERIALS

| | ITEM | SIZE | QTY | PRICE |
|---|---|---|---|---|
| ☐ | | | | |
| ☐ | | | | |
| ☐ | | | | |
| ☐ | | | | |
| ☐ | | | | |

## ADDITIONAL NOTES

PROJECT SKETCH / PHOTO

| | FILE/PROJECT NAME | | |
|---|---|---|---|
| | ORDER DATE | | WHERE ORDERED |
| | FILE COST | | CLIENT |
| | LASER ACTION | SCORE ☐ | ENGRAVE ☐    CUT ☐ |
| | RUN TIME | | ✔ FINISHED |

## SET-UP

| | MACHINE USED | | |
|---|---|---|---|
| | SETTINGS | SPEED | POWER        LPI |
| | NO. OF PASSES | | |
| | MATERIAL SIZE | | ▌▌▌ THICKNESS |

## MATERIALS

| | ITEM | SIZE | QTY | PRICE |
|---|---|---|---|---|
| ☐ | | | | |
| ☐ | | | | |
| ☐ | | | | |
| ☐ | | | | |
| ☐ | | | | |

## ADDITIONAL NOTES

| |
|---|
| |
| |
| |
| |

PROJECT SKETCH / PHOTO

| | FILE/PROJECT NAME | | |
| --- | --- | --- | --- |
| | ORDER DATE | | WHERE ORDERED |
| | FILE COST | | CLIENT |
| | LASER ACTION | SCORE ☐ | ENGRAVE ☐ CUT ☐ |
| | RUN TIME | | ✔ FINISHED |

## SET-UP

| | | | | |
| --- | --- | --- | --- | --- |
| | MACHINE USED | | | |
| | SETTINGS | SPEED | POWER | LPI |
| | NO. OF PASSES | | | |
| | MATERIAL SIZE | | THICKNESS | |

## MATERIALS

| | ITEM | SIZE | QTY | PRICE |
| --- | --- | --- | --- | --- |
| ☐ | | | | |
| ☐ | | | | |
| ☐ | | | | |
| ☐ | | | | |
| ☐ | | | | |

## ADDITIONAL NOTES

| |
| --- |
| |
| |
| |
| |

## PROJECT SKETCH / PHOTO

| | FILE/PROJECT NAME | | |
|---|---|---|---|
| | ORDER DATE | | WHERE ORDERED |
| | FILE COST | | CLIENT |
| | LASER ACTION | SCORE ☐ | ENGRAVE ☐  CUT ☐ |
| | RUN TIME | | ✔ FINISHED |

## SET-UP

| | MACHINE USED | | |
|---|---|---|---|
| | SETTINGS | SPEED | POWER  LPI |
| | NO. OF PASSES | | |
| | MATERIAL SIZE | | THICKNESS |

## MATERIALS

| | ITEM | SIZE | QTY | PRICE |
|---|---|---|---|---|
| ☐ | | | | |
| ☐ | | | | |
| ☐ | | | | |
| ☐ | | | | |
| ☐ | | | | |

## ADDITIONAL NOTES

| |
|---|
| |
| |
| |
| |

PROJECT SKETCH / PHOTO

| | FILE/PROJECT NAME | | |
|---|---|---|---|
| | ORDER DATE | | WHERE ORDERED |
| | FILE COST | | CLIENT |
| | LASER ACTION | SCORE ☐ | ENGRAVE ☐ CUT ☐ |
| | RUN TIME | | ✔ FINISHED |

## SET-UP

| | MACHINE USED | | |
|---|---|---|---|
| | SETTINGS | SPEED | POWER LPI |
| | NO. OF PASSES | | |
| | MATERIAL SIZE | | THICKNESS |

## MATERIALS

| | ITEM | SIZE | QTY | PRICE |
|---|---|---|---|---|
| ☐ | | | | |
| ☐ | | | | |
| ☐ | | | | |
| ☐ | | | | |
| ☐ | | | | |

## ADDITIONAL NOTES

| |
|---|
| |
| |
| |
| |
| |

PROJECT SKETCH / PHOTO

| | FILE/PROJECT NAME | |
|---|---|---|
| | ORDER DATE | WHERE ORDERED |
| | FILE COST | CLIENT |
| | LASER ACTION | SCORE ☐   ENGRAVE ☐   CUT ☐ |
| | RUN TIME | ✔ FINISHED |

## SET-UP

| | MACHINE USED | | |
|---|---|---|---|
| | SETTINGS | SPEED   POWER   LPI |
| | NO. OF PASSES | |
| | MATERIAL SIZE | THICKNESS |

## MATERIALS

| | ITEM | SIZE | QTY | PRICE |
|---|---|---|---|---|
| ☐ | | | | |
| ☐ | | | | |
| ☐ | | | | |
| ☐ | | | | |
| ☐ | | | | |

## ADDITIONAL NOTES

| |
|---|
| |
| |
| |
| |
| |

PROJECT SKETCH / PHOTO

| | FILE/PROJECT NAME | | | |
|---|---|---|---|---|
| | ORDER DATE | | WHERE ORDERED | |
| | FILE COST | | CLIENT | |
| | LASER ACTION | SCORE ☐ | ENGRAVE ☐ | CUT ☐ |
| | RUN TIME | | ✔ FINISHED | |

## SET-UP

| | | | | |
|---|---|---|---|---|
| | MACHINE USED | | | |
| | SETTINGS | SPEED | POWER | LPI |
| | NO. OF PASSES | | | |
| | MATERIAL SIZE | | THICKNESS | |

## MATERIALS

| | ITEM | SIZE | QTY | PRICE |
|---|---|---|---|---|
| ☐ | | | | |
| ☐ | | | | |
| ☐ | | | | |
| ☐ | | | | |
| ☐ | | | | |

## ADDITIONAL NOTES

| |
|---|
| |
| |
| |
| |
| |

PROJECT SKETCH / PHOTO

| | FILE/PROJECT NAME | | |
|---|---|---|---|
| | ORDER DATE | | WHERE ORDERED |
| | FILE COST | | CLIENT |
| | LASER ACTION | SCORE ☐ | ENGRAVE ☐   CUT ☐ |
| | RUN TIME | | ✔ FINISHED |

## SET-UP

| | | | | |
|---|---|---|---|---|
| | MACHINE USED | | | |
| | SETTINGS | SPEED | POWER | LPI |
| | NO. OF PASSES | | | |
| | MATERIAL SIZE | | THICKNESS | |

## MATERIALS

| | ITEM | SIZE | QTY | PRICE |
|---|---|---|---|---|
| ☐ | | | | |
| ☐ | | | | |
| ☐ | | | | |
| ☐ | | | | |
| ☐ | | | | |

## ADDITIONAL NOTES

| |
|---|
| |
| |
| |
| |
| |

PROJECT SKETCH / PHOTO

| | FILE/PROJECT NAME | | |
|---|---|---|---|
| | ORDER DATE | | WHERE ORDERED |
| | FILE COST | | CLIENT |
| | LASER ACTION | SCORE ☐ | ENGRAVE ☐ | CUT ☐ |
| | RUN TIME | | ✔ FINISHED |

## SET-UP

| | MACHINE USED | | |
|---|---|---|---|
| | SETTINGS | SPEED | POWER | LPI |
| | NO. OF PASSES | | |
| | MATERIAL SIZE | | THICKNESS |

## MATERIALS

| | ITEM | SIZE | QTY | PRICE |
|---|---|---|---|---|
| ☐ | | | | |
| ☐ | | | | |
| ☐ | | | | |
| ☐ | | | | |
| ☐ | | | | |

## ADDITIONAL NOTES

| |
|---|
| |
| |
| |
| |
| |

PROJECT SKETCH / PHOTO

| | FILE/PROJECT NAME | | |
|---|---|---|---|
| | ORDER DATE | | WHERE ORDERED |
| | FILE COST | | CLIENT |
| | LASER ACTION | SCORE ☐ | ENGRAVE ☐     CUT ☐ |
| | RUN TIME | | ✔ FINISHED |

## SET-UP

| | MACHINE USED | | |
|---|---|---|---|
| | SETTINGS | SPEED    POWER    LPI | |
| | NO. OF PASSES | | |
| | MATERIAL SIZE | | THICKNESS |

## MATERIALS

| | ITEM | SIZE | QTY | PRICE |
|---|---|---|---|---|
| ☐ | | | | |
| ☐ | | | | |
| ☐ | | | | |
| ☐ | | | | |
| ☐ | | | | |

## ADDITIONAL NOTES

| |
|---|
| |
| |
| |
| |
| |

**PROJECT SKETCH / PHOTO**

| | FILE/PROJECT NAME | | | |
|---|---|---|---|---|
| | ORDER DATE | | WHERE ORDERED | |
| | FILE COST | | CLIENT | |
| | LASER ACTION | SCORE ☐ | ENGRAVE ☐ | CUT ☐ |
| | RUN TIME | | ✔ FINISHED | |

## SET-UP

| | | | | |
|---|---|---|---|---|
| | MACHINE USED | | | |
| | SETTINGS | SPEED | POWER | LPI |
| | NO. OF PASSES | | | |
| | MATERIAL SIZE | | THICKNESS | |

## MATERIALS

| | ITEM | SIZE | QTY | PRICE |
|---|---|---|---|---|
| ☐ | | | | |
| ☐ | | | | |
| ☐ | | | | |
| ☐ | | | | |
| ☐ | | | | |

## ADDITIONAL NOTES

| |
|---|
| |
| |
| |
| |
| |

**PROJECT SKETCH / PHOTO**

| | FILE/PROJECT NAME | |
|---|---|---|
| | ORDER DATE | WHERE ORDERED |
| | FILE COST | CLIENT |
| | LASER ACTION | SCORE ☐  ENGRAVE ☐  CUT ☐ |
| | RUN TIME | ✔ FINISHED |

## SET-UP

| | MACHINE USED | | |
|---|---|---|---|
| | SETTINGS | SPEED  POWER  LPI |
| | NO. OF PASSES | |
| | MATERIAL SIZE | THICKNESS |

## MATERIALS

| | ITEM | SIZE | QTY | PRICE |
|---|---|---|---|---|
| ☐ | | | | |
| ☐ | | | | |
| ☐ | | | | |
| ☐ | | | | |
| ☐ | | | | |

## ADDITIONAL NOTES

PROJECT SKETCH / PHOTO

| | FILE/PROJECT NAME | | |
|---|---|---|---|
| | ORDER DATE | | WHERE ORDERED |
| | FILE COST | | CLIENT |
| | LASER ACTION | SCORE ☐ | ENGRAVE ☐    CUT ☐ |
| | RUN TIME | | ✔ FINISHED |

## SET-UP

| | MACHINE USED | | |
|---|---|---|---|
| | SETTINGS | SPEED | POWER    LPI |
| | NO. OF PASSES | | |
| | MATERIAL SIZE | | ▌▌▌ THICKNESS |

## MATERIALS

| | ITEM | SIZE | QTY | PRICE |
|---|---|---|---|---|
| ☐ | | | | |
| ☐ | | | | |
| ☐ | | | | |
| ☐ | | | | |
| ☐ | | | | |

## ADDITIONAL NOTES

PROJECT SKETCH / PHOTO

| | FILE/PROJECT NAME | |
|---|---|---|

| | ORDER DATE | | WHERE ORDERED |
|---|---|---|---|

| | FILE COST | | CLIENT |
|---|---|---|---|

| | LASER ACTION | SCORE ☐ | ENGRAVE ☐ | CUT ☐ |
|---|---|---|---|---|

| | RUN TIME | ✔ FINISHED |
|---|---|---|

## SET-UP

| | MACHINE USED | | | |
|---|---|---|---|---|
| | SETTINGS | SPEED | POWER | LPI |
| | NO. OF PASSES | | | |
| | MATERIAL SIZE | | THICKNESS | |

## MATERIALS

| | ITEM | SIZE | QTY | PRICE |
|---|---|---|---|---|
| ☐ | | | | |
| ☐ | | | | |
| ☐ | | | | |
| ☐ | | | | |
| ☐ | | | | |

## ADDITIONAL NOTES

| |
|---|
| |
| |
| |
| |

| | FILE/PROJECT NAME |
|---|---|

| | ORDER DATE | | WHERE ORDERED |
|---|---|---|---|
| | FILE COST | | CLIENT |

| | LASER ACTION | SCORE ☐ | ENGRAVE ☐ | CUT ☐ |
|---|---|---|---|---|

| | RUN TIME | ✔ FINISHED |
|---|---|---|

## SET-UP

| | MACHINE USED | | |
|---|---|---|---|
| | SETTINGS | SPEED | POWER | LPI |
| | NO. OF PASSES | | |
| | MATERIAL SIZE | THICKNESS | |

## MATERIALS

| | ITEM | SIZE | QTY | PRICE |
|---|---|---|---|---|
| ☐ | | | | |
| ☐ | | | | |
| ☐ | | | | |
| ☐ | | | | |
| ☐ | | | | |

## ADDITIONAL NOTES

| |
|---|
| |
| |
| |
| |

PROJECT SKETCH / PHOTO

| | FILE/PROJECT NAME | |
|---|---|---|

| | ORDER DATE | | WHERE ORDERED |
|---|---|---|---|

| | FILE COST | | CLIENT |
|---|---|---|---|

| | LASER ACTION | SCORE ☐ | ENGRAVE ☐ | CUT ☐ |
|---|---|---|---|---|

| | RUN TIME | ✔ FINISHED |
|---|---|---|

## SET-UP

| | MACHINE USED | | |
|---|---|---|---|
| | SETTINGS | SPEED | POWER | LPI |
| | NO. OF PASSES | | |
| | MATERIAL SIZE | THICKNESS | |

## MATERIALS

| | ITEM | SIZE | QTY | PRICE |
|---|---|---|---|---|
| ☐ | | | | |
| ☐ | | | | |
| ☐ | | | | |
| ☐ | | | | |
| ☐ | | | | |

## ADDITIONAL NOTES

PROJECT SKETCH / PHOTO

| | FILE/PROJECT NAME | | |
|---|---|---|---|
| | ORDER DATE | | WHERE ORDERED |
| | FILE COST | | CLIENT |
| | LASER ACTION | SCORE ☐ | ENGRAVE ☐   CUT ☐ |
| | RUN TIME | | ✔ FINISHED |

## SET-UP

| | | | |
|---|---|---|---|
| | MACHINE USED | | |
| | SETTINGS | SPEED | POWER   LPI |
| | NO. OF PASSES | | |
| | MATERIAL SIZE | | THICKNESS |

## MATERIALS

| | ITEM | SIZE | QTY | PRICE |
|---|---|---|---|---|
| ☐ | | | | |
| ☐ | | | | |
| ☐ | | | | |
| ☐ | | | | |
| ☐ | | | | |

## ADDITIONAL NOTES

| |
|---|
| |
| |
| |
| |
| |

PROJECT SKETCH / PHOTO

| | FILE/PROJECT NAME | | |
|---|---|---|---|

| | ORDER DATE | | WHERE ORDERED |
|---|---|---|---|

| | FILE COST | | CLIENT |
|---|---|---|---|

| | LASER ACTION | SCORE ☐ | ENGRAVE ☐ | CUT ☐ |

| | RUN TIME | ✔ FINISHED |

## SET-UP

| | MACHINE USED | | |
|---|---|---|---|
| | SETTINGS | SPEED | POWER | LPI |
| | NO. OF PASSES | | |
| | MATERIAL SIZE | THICKNESS |

## MATERIALS

| | ITEM | SIZE | QTY | PRICE |
|---|---|---|---|---|
| ☐ | | | | |
| ☐ | | | | |
| ☐ | | | | |
| ☐ | | | | |
| ☐ | | | | |

## ADDITIONAL NOTES

| |
|---|
| |
| |
| |
| |

PROJECT SKETCH / PHOTO

| | FILE/PROJECT NAME | | |
|---|---|---|---|
| | ORDER DATE | | WHERE ORDERED |
| | FILE COST | | CLIENT |
| | LASER ACTION | SCORE ☐ | ENGRAVE ☐ | CUT ☐ |
| | RUN TIME | | ✔ FINISHED |

## SET-UP

| | MACHINE USED | | |
|---|---|---|---|
| | SETTINGS | SPEED | POWER | LPI |
| | NO. OF PASSES | | |
| | MATERIAL SIZE | | THICKNESS |

## MATERIALS

| | ITEM | SIZE | QTY | PRICE |
|---|---|---|---|---|
| ☐ | | | | |
| ☐ | | | | |
| ☐ | | | | |
| ☐ | | | | |
| ☐ | | | | |

## ADDITIONAL NOTES

| |
|---|
| |
| |
| |
| |
| |

PROJECT SKETCH / PHOTO

| | FILE/PROJECT NAME | | |
|---|---|---|---|
| | ORDER DATE | | WHERE ORDERED |
| | FILE COST | | CLIENT |
| | LASER ACTION | SCORE ☐ | ENGRAVE ☐   CUT ☐ |
| | RUN TIME | | ✔ FINISHED |

## SET-UP

| | MACHINE USED | | |
|---|---|---|---|
| | SETTINGS | SPEED | POWER     LPI |
| | NO. OF PASSES | | |
| | MATERIAL SIZE | | THICKNESS |

## MATERIALS

| | ITEM | SIZE | QTY | PRICE |
|---|---|---|---|---|
| ☐ | | | | |
| ☐ | | | | |
| ☐ | | | | |
| ☐ | | | | |
| ☐ | | | | |

## ADDITIONAL NOTES

| |
|---|
| |
| |
| |
| |
| |

PROJECT SKETCH / PHOTO

| | FILE/PROJECT NAME | |
|---|---|---|
| | ORDER DATE | WHERE ORDERED |
| | FILE COST | CLIENT |
| | LASER ACTION SCORE ☐ | ENGRAVE ☐ CUT ☐ |
| | RUN TIME | ✔ FINISHED |

## SET-UP

| | | | | |
|---|---|---|---|---|
| | MACHINE USED | | | |
| | SETTINGS | SPEED | POWER | LPI |
| | NO. OF PASSES | | | |
| | MATERIAL SIZE | THICKNESS | | |

## MATERIALS

| | ITEM | SIZE | QTY | PRICE |
|---|---|---|---|---|
| ☐ | | | | |
| ☐ | | | | |
| ☐ | | | | |
| ☐ | | | | |
| ☐ | | | | |

## ADDITIONAL NOTES

| |
|---|
| |
| |
| |
| |
| |

## PROJECT SKETCH / PHOTO

| | FILE/PROJECT NAME | | |
|---|---|---|---|
| | ORDER DATE | | WHERE ORDERED |
| | FILE COST | | CLIENT |
| | LASER ACTION | SCORE ☐ | ENGRAVE ☐ CUT ☐ |
| | RUN TIME | | ✔ FINISHED |

## SET-UP

| | | | | |
|---|---|---|---|---|
| | MACHINE USED | | | |
| | SETTINGS | SPEED | POWER | LPI |
| | NO. OF PASSES | | | |
| | MATERIAL SIZE | | THICKNESS | |

## MATERIALS

| | ITEM | SIZE | QTY | PRICE |
|---|---|---|---|---|
| ☐ | | | | |
| ☐ | | | | |
| ☐ | | | | |
| ☐ | | | | |
| ☐ | | | | |

## ADDITIONAL NOTES

| |
|---|
| |
| |
| |
| |
| |

PROJECT SKETCH / PHOTO

## FILE/PROJECT NAME

| | |
|---|---|
| ORDER DATE | WHERE ORDERED |
| FILE COST | CLIENT |

LASER ACTION    SCORE ☐    ENGRAVE ☐    CUT ☐

RUN TIME    ✔ FINISHED

## SET-UP

MACHINE USED

SETTINGS    SPEED    POWER    LPI

NO. OF PASSES

MATERIAL SIZE    ||| THICKNESS

## MATERIALS

| | ITEM | SIZE | QTY | PRICE |
|---|---|---|---|---|
| ☐ | | | | |
| ☐ | | | | |
| ☐ | | | | |
| ☐ | | | | |
| ☐ | | | | |

## ADDITIONAL NOTES

| | FILE/PROJECT NAME | | |
|---|---|---|---|
| | ORDER DATE | | WHERE ORDERED |
| | FILE COST | | CLIENT |
| | LASER ACTION | SCORE ☐ | ENGRAVE ☐ CUT ☐ |
| | RUN TIME | | ✔ FINISHED |

## SET-UP

| | MACHINE USED | | |
|---|---|---|---|
| | SETTINGS | SPEED | POWER | LPI |
| | NO. OF PASSES | | |
| | MATERIAL SIZE | | ▮▮ THICKNESS |

## MATERIALS

| | ITEM | SIZE | QTY | PRICE |
|---|---|---|---|---|
| ☐ | | | | |
| ☐ | | | | |
| ☐ | | | | |
| ☐ | | | | |
| ☐ | | | | |

## ADDITIONAL NOTES

| |
|---|
| |
| |
| |
| |

PROJECT SKETCH / PHOTO

## FILE/PROJECT NAME

| | |
|---|---|
| ORDER DATE | WHERE ORDERED |
| FILE COST | CLIENT |

LASER ACTION    SCORE ☐    ENGRAVE ☐    CUT ☐

RUN TIME    ✔ FINISHED

## SET-UP

MACHINE USED

SETTINGS    SPEED    POWER    LPI

NO. OF PASSES

MATERIAL SIZE    ||| THICKNESS

## MATERIALS

| | ITEM | SIZE | QTY | PRICE |
|---|---|---|---|---|
| ☐ | | | | |
| ☐ | | | | |
| ☐ | | | | |
| ☐ | | | | |
| ☐ | | | | |

## ADDITIONAL NOTES

PROJECT SKETCH / PHOTO

| FILE/PROJECT NAME | |
|---|---|
| ORDER DATE | WHERE ORDERED |
| FILE COST | CLIENT |
| LASER ACTION  SCORE ☐ | ENGRAVE ☐  CUT ☐ |
| RUN TIME | ✔ FINISHED |

## SET-UP

| MACHINE USED | | |
|---|---|---|
| SETTINGS | SPEED  POWER | LPI |
| NO. OF PASSES | | |
| MATERIAL SIZE | ▦ THICKNESS | |

## MATERIALS

| | ITEM | SIZE | QTY | PRICE |
|---|---|---|---|---|
| ☐ | | | | |
| ☐ | | | | |
| ☐ | | | | |
| ☐ | | | | |
| ☐ | | | | |

## ADDITIONAL NOTES

| |
|---|
| |
| |
| |
| |
| |

PROJECT SKETCH / PHOTO

| | FILE/PROJECT NAME | |
|---|---|---|

| | ORDER DATE | | WHERE ORDERED |
|---|---|---|---|

| | FILE COST | | CLIENT |
|---|---|---|---|

**LASER ACTION**  SCORE ☐  ENGRAVE ☐  CUT ☐

| | RUN TIME | ✔ FINISHED |
|---|---|---|

## SET-UP

**MACHINE USED**

**SETTINGS**  SPEED  POWER  LPI

**NO. OF PASSES**

**MATERIAL SIZE**  THICKNESS

## MATERIALS

| | ITEM | SIZE | QTY | PRICE |
|---|---|---|---|---|
| ☐ | | | | |
| ☐ | | | | |
| ☐ | | | | |
| ☐ | | | | |
| ☐ | | | | |

## ADDITIONAL NOTES

PROJECT SKETCH / PHOTO

| | FILE/PROJECT NAME | | | | |
|---|---|---|---|---|---|
| | ORDER DATE | | WHERE ORDERED | | |
| | FILE COST | | CLIENT | | |
| | LASER ACTION | SCORE ☐ | ENGRAVE ☐ | | CUT ☐ |
| | RUN TIME | | ✔ FINISHED | | |

## SET-UP

| | MACHINE USED | | | |
|---|---|---|---|---|
| | SETTINGS | SPEED | POWER | LPI |
| | NO. OF PASSES | | | |
| | MATERIAL SIZE | | ▌▌▌ THICKNESS | |

## MATERIALS

| | ITEM | SIZE | QTY | PRICE |
|---|---|---|---|---|
| ☐ | | | | |
| ☐ | | | | |
| ☐ | | | | |
| ☐ | | | | |
| ☐ | | | | |

## ADDITIONAL NOTES

| |
|---|
| |
| |
| |
| |
| |

PROJECT SKETCH / PHOTO

| | FILE/PROJECT NAME | | |
|---|---|---|---|

| | ORDER DATE | | WHERE ORDERED |
|---|---|---|---|

| | FILE COST | | CLIENT |
|---|---|---|---|

| | LASER ACTION | SCORE ☐ | ENGRAVE ☐ | CUT ☐ |
|---|---|---|---|---|

| | RUN TIME | | ✔ FINISHED |
|---|---|---|---|

## SET-UP

| | MACHINE USED | | |
|---|---|---|---|

| | SETTINGS | SPEED | POWER | LPI |
|---|---|---|---|---|

| | NO. OF PASSES | | |
|---|---|---|---|

| | MATERIAL SIZE | | THICKNESS |
|---|---|---|---|

## MATERIALS

| | ITEM | SIZE | QTY | PRICE |
|---|---|---|---|---|
| ☐ | | | | |
| ☐ | | | | |
| ☐ | | | | |
| ☐ | | | | |
| ☐ | | | | |

## ADDITIONAL NOTES

PROJECT SKETCH / PHOTO

| | FILE/PROJECT NAME | | |
|---|---|---|---|
| | ORDER DATE | | WHERE ORDERED |
| | FILE COST | | CLIENT |
| | LASER ACTION | SCORE ☐ | ENGRAVE ☐    CUT ☐ |
| | RUN TIME | | ✔ FINISHED |

## SET-UP

| | | | |
|---|---|---|---|
| | MACHINE USED | | |
| | SETTINGS | SPEED    POWER | LPI |
| | NO. OF PASSES | | |
| | MATERIAL SIZE | | THICKNESS |

## MATERIALS

| | ITEM | SIZE | QTY | PRICE |
|---|---|---|---|---|
| ☐ | | | | |
| ☐ | | | | |
| ☐ | | | | |
| ☐ | | | | |
| ☐ | | | | |

## ADDITIONAL NOTES

| |
|---|
| |
| |
| |
| |
| |

PROJECT SKETCH / PHOTO

| | FILE/PROJECT NAME | | |
|---|---|---|---|
| | ORDER DATE | | WHERE ORDERED |
| | FILE COST | | CLIENT |
| | LASER ACTION | SCORE ☐ | ENGRAVE ☐     CUT ☐ |
| | RUN TIME | | ✔ FINISHED |

## SET-UP

| | MACHINE USED | | | |
|---|---|---|---|---|
| | SETTINGS | SPEED | POWER | LPI |
| | NO. OF PASSES | | | |
| | MATERIAL SIZE | | ▐▌▐ THICKNESS | |

## MATERIALS

| | ITEM | SIZE | QTY | PRICE |
|---|---|---|---|---|
| ☐ | | | | |
| ☐ | | | | |
| ☐ | | | | |
| ☐ | | | | |
| ☐ | | | | |

## ADDITIONAL NOTES

| |
|---|
| |
| |
| |
| |

PROJECT SKETCH / PHOTO

| | FILE/PROJECT NAME | | |
|---|---|---|---|

| | ORDER DATE | | WHERE ORDERED |
|---|---|---|---|
| | FILE COST | | CLIENT |
| | LASER ACTION | SCORE ☐  ENGRAVE ☐ | CUT ☐ |
| | RUN TIME | | ✔ FINISHED |

## SET-UP

| | MACHINE USED | | | |
|---|---|---|---|---|
| | SETTINGS | SPEED | POWER | LPI |
| | NO. OF PASSES | | | |
| | MATERIAL SIZE | | THICKNESS | |

## MATERIALS

| | ITEM | SIZE | QTY | PRICE |
|---|---|---|---|---|
| ☐ | | | | |
| ☐ | | | | |
| ☐ | | | | |
| ☐ | | | | |
| ☐ | | | | |

## ADDITIONAL NOTES

| |
|---|
| |
| |
| |
| |

PROJECT SKETCH / PHOTO

| | FILE/PROJECT NAME | | |
|---|---|---|---|
| | ORDER DATE | | WHERE ORDERED |
| | FILE COST | | CLIENT |
| | LASER ACTION | SCORE ☐ | ENGRAVE ☐ CUT ☐ |
| | RUN TIME | | ✔ FINISHED |

## SET-UP

| | MACHINE USED | | | |
|---|---|---|---|---|
| | SETTINGS | SPEED | POWER | LPI |
| | NO. OF PASSES | | | |
| | MATERIAL SIZE | | THICKNESS | |

## MATERIALS

| | ITEM | SIZE | QTY | PRICE |
|---|---|---|---|---|
| ☐ | | | | |
| ☐ | | | | |
| ☐ | | | | |
| ☐ | | | | |
| ☐ | | | | |

## ADDITIONAL NOTES

| |
|---|
| |
| |
| |
| |
| |

PROJECT SKETCH / PHOTO

| | FILE/PROJECT NAME | | |
|---|---|---|---|

| | ORDER DATE | | WHERE ORDERED |
|---|---|---|---|

| | FILE COST | | CLIENT |
|---|---|---|---|

| | LASER ACTION | SCORE ☐ | ENGRAVE ☐ | CUT ☐ |
|---|---|---|---|---|

| | RUN TIME | ✔ FINISHED |
|---|---|---|

## SET-UP

| | MACHINE USED | | | |
|---|---|---|---|---|
| | SETTINGS | SPEED | POWER | LPI |
| | NO. OF PASSES | | | |
| | MATERIAL SIZE | THICKNESS | | |

## MATERIALS

| | ITEM | SIZE | QTY | PRICE |
|---|---|---|---|---|
| ☐ | | | | |
| ☐ | | | | |
| ☐ | | | | |
| ☐ | | | | |
| ☐ | | | | |

## ADDITIONAL NOTES

| |
|---|
| |
| |
| |
| |

PROJECT SKETCH / PHOTO

| | FILE/PROJECT NAME | |
|---|---|---|
| | ORDER DATE | WHERE ORDERED |
| | FILE COST | CLIENT |
| | LASER ACTION | SCORE ☐    ENGRAVE ☐    CUT ☐ |
| | RUN TIME | ✔ FINISHED |

## SET-UP

| | MACHINE USED | | |
|---|---|---|---|
| | SETTINGS | SPEED | POWER | LPI |
| | NO. OF PASSES | | |
| | MATERIAL SIZE | ▌▌ THICKNESS | |

## MATERIALS

| | ITEM | SIZE | QTY | PRICE |
|---|---|---|---|---|
| ☐ | | | | |
| ☐ | | | | |
| ☐ | | | | |
| ☐ | | | | |
| ☐ | | | | |

## ADDITIONAL NOTES

| |
|---|
| |
| |
| |
| |

PROJECT SKETCH / PHOTO

| | FILE/PROJECT NAME | | |
|---|---|---|---|
| | ORDER DATE | | WHERE ORDERED |
| | FILE COST | | CLIENT |
| | LASER ACTION | SCORE ☐ | ENGRAVE ☐ CUT ☐ |
| | RUN TIME | | ✔ FINISHED |

## SET-UP

| | MACHINE USED | | | |
|---|---|---|---|---|
| | SETTINGS | SPEED | POWER | LPI |
| | NO. OF PASSES | | | |
| | MATERIAL SIZE | | THICKNESS | |

## MATERIALS

| | ITEM | SIZE | QTY | PRICE |
|---|---|---|---|---|
| ☐ | | | | |
| ☐ | | | | |
| ☐ | | | | |
| ☐ | | | | |
| ☐ | | | | |

## ADDITIONAL NOTES

| |
|---|
| |
| |
| |
| |
| |

PROJECT SKETCH / PHOTO

| | FILE/PROJECT NAME | | |
|---|---|---|---|

| ORDER DATE | | WHERE ORDERED |
|---|---|---|

| FILE COST | | CLIENT |
|---|---|---|

| LASER ACTION | SCORE ☐ | ENGRAVE ☐ | CUT ☐ |
|---|---|---|---|

| RUN TIME | | ✔ FINISHED |
|---|---|---|

## SET-UP

| MACHINE USED | | | |
|---|---|---|---|

| SETTINGS | SPEED | POWER | LPI |
|---|---|---|---|

| NO. OF PASSES | | | |
|---|---|---|---|

| MATERIAL SIZE | | THICKNESS |
|---|---|---|

## MATERIALS

| | ITEM | SIZE | QTY | PRICE |
|---|---|---|---|---|
| ☐ | | | | |
| ☐ | | | | |
| ☐ | | | | |
| ☐ | | | | |
| ☐ | | | | |

## ADDITIONAL NOTES

| |
|---|
| |
| |
| |
| |

PROJECT SKETCH / PHOTO

| | FILE/PROJECT NAME | | |
|---|---|---|---|
| | ORDER DATE | | WHERE ORDERED |
| | FILE COST | | CLIENT |
| | LASER ACTION | SCORE ☐ | ENGRAVE ☐ | CUT ☐ |
| | RUN TIME | | ✔ FINISHED |

## SET-UP

| | MACHINE USED | | |
|---|---|---|---|
| | SETTINGS | SPEED | POWER | LPI |
| | NO. OF PASSES | | |
| | MATERIAL SIZE | | ▌▌▌ THICKNESS |

## MATERIALS

| | ITEM | SIZE | QTY | PRICE |
|---|---|---|---|---|
| ☐ | | | | |
| ☐ | | | | |
| ☐ | | | | |
| ☐ | | | | |
| ☐ | | | | |

## ADDITIONAL NOTES

| |
|---|
| |
| |
| |
| |
| |

| | FILE/PROJECT NAME | | |
|---|---|---|---|
| | ORDER DATE | | WHERE ORDERED |
| | FILE COST | | CLIENT |
| | LASER ACTION | SCORE ☐ | ENGRAVE ☐ | CUT ☐ |
| | RUN TIME | | ✔ FINISHED |

## SET-UP

| | MACHINE USED | | |
|---|---|---|---|
| | SETTINGS | SPEED | POWER | LPI |
| | NO. OF PASSES | | |
| | MATERIAL SIZE | | THICKNESS |

## MATERIALS

| | ITEM | SIZE | QTY | PRICE |
|---|---|---|---|---|
| ☐ | | | | |
| ☐ | | | | |
| ☐ | | | | |
| ☐ | | | | |
| ☐ | | | | |

## ADDITIONAL NOTES

PROJECT SKETCH / PHOTO

| | FILE/PROJECT NAME | | |
|---|---|---|---|
| | ORDER DATE | | WHERE ORDERED |
| | FILE COST | | CLIENT |
| | LASER ACTION | SCORE ☐ | ENGRAVE ☐ | CUT ☐ |
| | RUN TIME | | ✔ FINISHED |

## SET-UP

| | | | |
|---|---|---|---|
| | MACHINE USED | | |
| | SETTINGS | SPEED | POWER | LPI |
| | NO. OF PASSES | | |
| | MATERIAL SIZE | | THICKNESS |

## MATERIALS

| | ITEM | SIZE | QTY | PRICE |
|---|---|---|---|---|
| ☐ | | | | |
| ☐ | | | | |
| ☐ | | | | |
| ☐ | | | | |
| ☐ | | | | |

## ADDITIONAL NOTES

PROJECT SKETCH / PHOTO

| | FILE/PROJECT NAME | | |
|---|---|---|---|
| | ORDER DATE | | WHERE ORDERED |
| | FILE COST | | CLIENT |
| | LASER ACTION | SCORE ☐    ENGRAVE ☐ | CUT ☐ |
| | RUN TIME | | ✔ FINISHED |

## SET-UP

| | MACHINE USED | | |
|---|---|---|---|
| | SETTINGS | SPEED | POWER | LPI |
| | NO. OF PASSES | | |
| | MATERIAL SIZE | | THICKNESS |

## MATERIALS

| | ITEM | SIZE | QTY | PRICE |
|---|---|---|---|---|
| ☐ | | | | |
| ☐ | | | | |
| ☐ | | | | |
| ☐ | | | | |
| ☐ | | | | |

## ADDITIONAL NOTES

| |
|---|
| |
| |
| |
| |

| | FILE/PROJECT NAME | | |
|---|---|---|---|
| | ORDER DATE | | WHERE ORDERED |
| | FILE COST | | CLIENT |
| | LASER ACTION | SCORE ☐ | ENGRAVE ☐ CUT ☐ |
| | RUN TIME | | ✔ FINISHED |

## SET-UP

| | | | | |
|---|---|---|---|---|
| | MACHINE USED | | | |
| | SETTINGS | SPEED | POWER | LPI |
| | NO. OF PASSES | | | |
| | MATERIAL SIZE | | THICKNESS | |

## MATERIALS

| | ITEM | SIZE | QTY | PRICE |
|---|---|---|---|---|
| ☐ | | | | |
| ☐ | | | | |
| ☐ | | | | |
| ☐ | | | | |
| ☐ | | | | |

## ADDITIONAL NOTES

| |
|---|
| |
| |
| |
| |
| |

PROJECT SKETCH / PHOTO

| | FILE/PROJECT NAME | |
|---|---|---|
| | ORDER DATE | WHERE ORDERED |
| | FILE COST | CLIENT |
| | LASER ACTION SCORE ☐ | ENGRAVE ☐ CUT ☐ |
| | RUN TIME | ✔ FINISHED |

## SET-UP

| | MACHINE USED | | |
|---|---|---|---|
| | SETTINGS SPEED | POWER | LPI |
| | NO. OF PASSES | | |
| | MATERIAL SIZE | THICKNESS | |

## MATERIALS

| | ITEM | SIZE | QTY | PRICE |
|---|---|---|---|---|
| ☐ | | | | |
| ☐ | | | | |
| ☐ | | | | |
| ☐ | | | | |
| ☐ | | | | |

## ADDITIONAL NOTES

| |
|---|
| |
| |
| |
| |

PROJECT SKETCH / PHOTO

| | FILE/PROJECT NAME |
|---|---|

| | ORDER DATE | | WHERE ORDERED |
|---|---|---|---|

| | FILE COST | | CLIENT |
|---|---|---|---|

LASER ACTION    SCORE ☐    ENGRAVE ☐    CUT ☐

| | RUN TIME | ✔ FINISHED |
|---|---|---|

## SET-UP

MACHINE USED

SETTINGS    SPEED    POWER    LPI

NO. OF PASSES

MATERIAL SIZE    ‖‖ THICKNESS

## MATERIALS

| | ITEM | SIZE | QTY | PRICE |
|---|---|---|---|---|
| ☐ | | | | |
| ☐ | | | | |
| ☐ | | | | |
| ☐ | | | | |
| ☐ | | | | |

## ADDITIONAL NOTES

| |
|---|
| |
| |
| |
| |

| | FILE/PROJECT NAME | | |
|---|---|---|---|

| | ORDER DATE | | WHERE ORDERED |
|---|---|---|---|

| | FILE COST | | CLIENT |
|---|---|---|---|

| | LASER ACTION | SCORE ☐ | ENGRAVE ☐ | CUT ☐ |
|---|---|---|---|---|

| | RUN TIME | ✔ FINISHED |
|---|---|---|

## SET-UP

| | MACHINE USED | | |
|---|---|---|---|
| | SETTINGS | SPEED | POWER | LPI |
| | NO. OF PASSES | | |
| | MATERIAL SIZE | THICKNESS |

## MATERIALS

| | ITEM | SIZE | QTY | PRICE |
|---|---|---|---|---|
| ☐ | | | | |
| ☐ | | | | |
| ☐ | | | | |
| ☐ | | | | |
| ☐ | | | | |

## ADDITIONAL NOTES

| |
|---|
| |
| |
| |
| |

PROJECT SKETCH / PHOTO

| | FILE/PROJECT NAME | | |
|---|---|---|---|
| | ORDER DATE | | WHERE ORDERED |
| | FILE COST | | CLIENT |
| | LASER ACTION | SCORE ☐ | ENGRAVE ☐ CUT ☐ |
| | RUN TIME | | ✔ FINISHED |

## SET-UP

| | MACHINE USED | | |
|---|---|---|---|
| | SETTINGS | SPEED | POWER | LPI |
| | NO. OF PASSES | | |
| | MATERIAL SIZE | | THICKNESS |

## MATERIALS

| | ITEM | SIZE | QTY | PRICE |
|---|---|---|---|---|
| ☐ | | | | |
| ☐ | | | | |
| ☐ | | | | |
| ☐ | | | | |
| ☐ | | | | |

## ADDITIONAL NOTES

PROJECT SKETCH / PHOTO

## FILE/PROJECT NAME

| | |
|---|---|
| ORDER DATE | WHERE ORDERED |
| FILE COST | CLIENT |
| LASER ACTION    SCORE ☐ | ENGRAVE ☐    CUT ☐ |
| RUN TIME | ✔ FINISHED |

## SET-UP

| | | | |
|---|---|---|---|
| MACHINE USED | | | |
| SETTINGS | SPEED | POWER | LPI |
| NO. OF PASSES | | | |
| MATERIAL SIZE | | ▌▌▌ THICKNESS | |

## MATERIALS

| | ITEM | SIZE | QTY | PRICE |
|---|---|---|---|---|
| ☐ | | | | |
| ☐ | | | | |
| ☐ | | | | |
| ☐ | | | | |
| ☐ | | | | |

## ADDITIONAL NOTES

| |
|---|
| |
| |
| |
| |

| | FILE/PROJECT NAME | | |
|---|---|---|---|

| | ORDER DATE | | WHERE ORDERED |
|---|---|---|---|

| | FILE COST | | CLIENT |
|---|---|---|---|

LASER ACTION — SCORE ☐ — ENGRAVE ☐ — CUT ☐

| | RUN TIME | ✔ FINISHED |
|---|---|---|

## SET-UP

| | MACHINE USED | | |
|---|---|---|---|
| | SETTINGS | SPEED — POWER — LPI | |
| | NO. OF PASSES | | |
| | MATERIAL SIZE | THICKNESS | |

## MATERIALS

| | ITEM | SIZE | QTY | PRICE |
|---|---|---|---|---|
| ☐ | | | | |
| ☐ | | | | |
| ☐ | | | | |
| ☐ | | | | |
| ☐ | | | | |

## ADDITIONAL NOTES

| |
|---|
| |
| |
| |
| |

PROJECT SKETCH / PHOTO

## FILE/PROJECT NAME

| | |
|---|---|
| ORDER DATE | WHERE ORDERED |
| FILE COST | CLIENT |

LASER ACTION  SCORE ☐  ENGRAVE ☐  CUT ☐

| | |
|---|---|
| RUN TIME | ✔ FINISHED |

## SET-UP

MACHINE USED

SETTINGS  SPEED  POWER  LPI

NO. OF PASSES

MATERIAL SIZE  ▌▌▌ THICKNESS

## MATERIALS

| | ITEM | SIZE | QTY | PRICE |
|---|---|---|---|---|
| ☐ | | | | |
| ☐ | | | | |
| ☐ | | | | |
| ☐ | | | | |
| ☐ | | | | |

## ADDITIONAL NOTES

PROJECT SKETCH / PHOTO

| | FILE/PROJECT NAME | | |
|---|---|---|---|
| | ORDER DATE | | WHERE ORDERED |
| | FILE COST | | CLIENT |
| | LASER ACTION | SCORE ☐ | ENGRAVE ☐  CUT ☐ |
| | RUN TIME | | ✔ FINISHED |

## SET-UP

| | | | | |
|---|---|---|---|---|
| | MACHINE USED | | | |
| | SETTINGS | SPEED | POWER | LPI |
| | NO. OF PASSES | | | |
| | MATERIAL SIZE | | THICKNESS | |

## MATERIALS

| | ITEM | SIZE | QTY | PRICE |
|---|---|---|---|---|
| ☐ | | | | |
| ☐ | | | | |
| ☐ | | | | |
| ☐ | | | | |
| ☐ | | | | |

## ADDITIONAL NOTES

| |
|---|
| |
| |
| |
| |
| |

| | FILE/PROJECT NAME | | |
|---|---|---|---|
| | ORDER DATE | | WHERE ORDERED |
| | FILE COST | | CLIENT |
| | LASER ACTION | SCORE ☐ | ENGRAVE ☐ | CUT ☐ |
| | RUN TIME | | ✔ FINISHED |

## SET-UP

| | MACHINE USED | | | |
|---|---|---|---|---|
| | SETTINGS | SPEED | POWER | LPI |
| | NO. OF PASSES | | | |
| | MATERIAL SIZE | | THICKNESS | |

## MATERIALS

| | ITEM | SIZE | QTY | PRICE |
|---|---|---|---|---|
| ☐ | | | | |
| ☐ | | | | |
| ☐ | | | | |
| ☐ | | | | |
| ☐ | | | | |

## ADDITIONAL NOTES

PROJECT SKETCH / PHOTO

| | FILE/PROJECT NAME | |
|---|---|---|
| | ORDER DATE | WHERE ORDERED |
| | FILE COST | CLIENT |
| | LASER ACTION    SCORE ☐ | ENGRAVE ☐    CUT ☐ |
| | RUN TIME | ✔ FINISHED |

## SET-UP

| | MACHINE USED | | |
|---|---|---|---|
| | SETTINGS | SPEED    POWER | LPI |
| | NO. OF PASSES | | |
| | MATERIAL SIZE | THICKNESS | |

## MATERIALS

| | ITEM | SIZE | QTY | PRICE |
|---|---|---|---|---|
| ☐ | | | | |
| ☐ | | | | |
| ☐ | | | | |
| ☐ | | | | |
| ☐ | | | | |

## ADDITIONAL NOTES

| |
|---|
| |
| |
| |
| |
| |

PROJECT SKETCH / PHOTO

Made in United States
Troutdale, OR
11/05/2024

24431921R00060